Eyemouth
in old picture postcards volume 2

by Lawson Wood

European Library   ZALTBOMMEL/THE NETHERLANDS

GB ISBN 90 288 6061 4 / CIP

© 1995 European Library – Zaltbommel/The Netherlands

No part of this book may be reproduced in any form, by print, photoprint, microfilm or any other means, without written permission from the publisher.

Introduction

Eyemouth, from her earliest mention in 1098 when King Edgar founded the Priory at Coldingham, was already an important port and the monks from the Priory retained land on the riverside in Eyemouth to facilitate the landing and storage of their supplies.

Eyemouth, or Emuth as she was originally called, is still the largest town in the area and has been at the forefront of British history when her fort on the promontary overlooking the 'roadsteads' was particularly mentioned in the Treaty of Boulogne. The Treaty stated that Eyemouth Fort had to be utterly destroyed as it was seen to be a threat to the tenuous peace held between Scotland, England and France. James VI visited the town and declared Eyemouth a Burgh of Barony in 1597 with the added privilege of being a free port.

This ensured that Eyemouth was now a Burgh in its own right and no longer under the control of Coldingham Priory. The town now enjoyed a booming period of free trade and was soon notorious for smuggling. By the turn of the following century, there was said to have been more of Eyemouth underground than there was above!

Gunsgreen House was the centre for much of this activity, with many of the rooms having secret passageways which extended to the vast storage cellars and on to the river bank. Early tales tell of passageways continuing around the coastline towards Burnmouth. The only Excise man ever welcomed in Eyemouth was Robert Burns, who stayed in the town in 1787.

Gunsgreen House was also involved in the conspiracy by the Earl of Gowrie to assassinate King James VI. The owner of the house at the time, Robert Logan of Restalrig, was also the laird of Fastcastle. He was described at the time as *'ane godles drunkin and deboshit man'* and suited the purposes of the Earl of Gowrie. The assassination attempt failed and it was not until a number of years later, after Robert Logan had died, that he was linked to the plot. His body was exumed and taken to the High Court. Robert Logan's remains were tried for treason and sentenced to death!

The Berwickshire coastal fishing villages still live under the shadow of the terrible disaster which hit the east coast on 14th October 1881. 'Black Friday', as it came to be known, saw the loss of 189 men during a sudden tempest. A constant reminder to this terror is the tapestry (now internationally famous) on permanent display in the Eyemouth Museum.

The creation of tithes on fishing also brought Eyemouth into the national headlines. The Eyemouth fishermen's views were openly hostile to this payment and demonstrations soon followed. Other fishermen along the entire British coast also took up the rally and William Spears of Eyemouth headed the delegation to challenge the authorities. Over 4,000 people marched to Ayton Castle in protest.

> *In liberty's ennobling cause,*
> *Our fisher lads stand weel,*
> *And gloriously have won the right*
> *Of freedom to the creel*

'Wullie Spears' was dubbed the King of Fishermen and died on 10th August 1885.

> *He died at Eyemouth, where for long*
> *His spear was aye in battle strong,*
> *But fought not he for strife,*
> *But for a point he thought was higher*
> *Than the summit of the auld kirk spire –*
> *A spark of heavenly life.*

Inexorably, Eyemouth's history and future are linked with her close neighbours: St. Abbs and Coldingham to the north, Burnmouth and Lamberton to the south. Of these four communities, two are situated on the coast and are also involved in the fishing industry, the other two are situated just inland.

St. Abbs was once known as 'Coldingham Shore' and started off as the closest port of call for Coldingham Priory. St. Abbs Head to the north was previously known as Coldburgh Head. The first St. Abbs lifeboat was the 'Helen Smitten', launched in 1911 as a direct result of the loss of the freighter 'Alfred Earlandson', which foundered on the treacherous Ebb Carrs to the south of St. Abbs harbour. Sadly, the only survivor was a dog.

It is interesting to note that the entire coastline from St. Abbs Head to Burnmouth is now a voluntary marine nature reserve and that the present day scuba divers now dive on the wreck of the Alfred Earlandson which was originally salvaged by the old 'hard-hat' divers.

Coldingham, once the seat of local government, is now a quiet, peaceful village. New housing developments have sadly altered the town's quaint aspect, but the Church of Coldingham Priory still dominates the town.

Built in 1098, it is a superb example of medieval crafsmenship and many of the original mason's tombs can still be seen in the old graveyard. Look for the skull and cross-bones. The original abbey was destroyed, but the church is still in use today and the acoustics inside are superb for choirs.

As you continue towards Eyemouth there is picturesque Coldingham Bay, rated as one of the top beaches in Europe, it started off as a very early Victorian resort. Eyemouth's beach disappears with each high tide! Burnmouth also has no beach. The town is actually split into four virtually separate villages. Upper Burnmouth at the top of the hill, Ross, Cowdrait and Partenhall 'doon the brae'. Burnmouth was of course the terminus for the Eyemouth Railway, which was opened in 1891. Burnmouth as an active station was eventually closed when the Eyemouth service on the branch line was terminated in 1962. Although the station is no longer in use, the main line railway still passes through.

The fishermen from Burnmouth's rocky shore are primarily lobster and crab fishermen. In fact the name of one of the settlements – Partenhall – is derived from the word 'parten', which is the local name for the common shore crab.

Lamberton village is now little more than a few farm cottages scattered along the old A1 route. Lamberton itself is no more. The buildings on the border with England have long since been demolished. Lamberton was once more important than Gretna Green for marriage ceremonies. In this, the second volume of 'Eyemouth in old picture postcards', I have uncovered a large number of interesting postcards and photographs. Although the prerequisite of the published material is for postcards before 1930, I have also included one photograph from the 1950's. This is of the 'Prefabs' next to the Toll Bridge. The 'Prefabs' have now long gone, but they are still there in the memory of the towns people.

Eyemouth and the border villages along the south east coast of Scotland still have a great deal to offer the visiting tourist and new tourism developments are planned for forthcoming years. I can only reiterate one of the quotes from the first book by a French general who was in the service of Mary Queen of Scots. He said: 'Keep your eyes on Eyemouth.'

Once more Eyemouth is undergoing a transition. A more modern harbour will be built shortly, new housing developments and recreational facilities are also planned.

Acknowledgements:
Eyemouth Museum
St. Abbs and Eyemouth Lifeboat Service.

Other reading:
Eyemouth in old picture postcards volume 1 by Lawson Wood
The Eight Minute Link, a History of the Eyemouth Railway by Lawson Wood
Berwick upon Tweed in old picture postcards by Lawson Wood
An old-time Fishing Town: Eyemouth – Its History, Romance and Tragedy by Daniel M'Ivor, 1906.

1   Early aerial photographs are always rare and this one is no exception. The photograph was part of a series taken all the way up the east coast. The scene is of Eyemouth before the promenade was built, before Gunsgreen was completed, there was no Caravan Park, Deanhead or Barefoots. Coldingham Road hadn't been fully developed and the gas works were still in operation.

2   Another aerial view, this time of the area at the north of the town. This is a much earlier photograph and depicts a scene before the housing scheme was built up Hurkur. The old Northburn Garage is there, but it used to be a church. You can see a funfair on the field next to Northburn Farm on the site where the swimming pool is now.

778. EYEMOUTH FROM THE AIR.

3   Northburn Farm and the old garage behind it. The road leading up to the fort is now completely changed and the only original buildings left from the farm is the farmhouse itself, although even this has changed somewhat in the passing years. This postcard was produced and distributed by J. Parker, 1 High Street, Eyemouth.

4   This wonderful old photograph produced as a very limited picture postcard for the mums of these young Eyemouth girls dancing group. The youngster in the middle is my mother, Barbara Wood. This was taken around 1925.

5   The field behind Northburn Farm next to the 'bantry' is now the site of Eyemouth's swimming pool and leisure centre. At one time it was run as a putting green and the building to the left was a wooden structure used for changing into your swimming attire for the beach: the ladies on one side, the gents on the other. Beach House is still there, but in this photograph, it quite clearly had two entrance halls and was obviously two separate houses at one time.

320.   THE PUTTING GREEN AND HARBOUR, EYEMOUTH.

6/7   These two postcards photographed at the same time show the entire stretch of Eyemouth beach and tell the story of 'bathing each morning before breakfast "no-kidding" '. This was posted to Glasgow on 20th July. This date is still traditionally used and is in the Glasgow Fair fortnight, still the last two weeks of July.

609. THE BEACH, EYEMOUTH, LOOKING NORTH.

The new promenade has yet to be built, as well as the new harbour entrance. You were once able to hire deckchairs for use on the beach and this must have been a particularly fine day, because the beach is packed with holidaymakers. There is a vendor selling ice-cream and a small boat is taking passengers for trips around the bay. The beach is still popular, but is completely covered at high tide.

8   On the promontory overlooking Eyemouth Bay or the 'roadsteads' as they are known, there was once a very famous fortress. Sadly nothing remains of the fort due to the fact that it was utterly destroyed in the sixteenth century. All of the old walls facing stones were removed and used in the construction of the Elizabethan walls at Berwick-upon-Tweed. What was left was used by Smeeton when he constructed the old harbour wall. This gun on its carriage also came from Berwick and was never fired in anger.

9   This is a very fine picture postcard showing Eyemouth's fishing fleet of Fifies waiting to enter the harbour due to the fact that the tide is too far out to negotiate the sand bars. These drifters, tightly packed, will resume the order with which they sailed into the bay. The first into the bay, the first into the harbour, with possibly the best price for their catch of fish.

10   Another very lovely photograph produced by R.A. McIvor and Son, the local chemist and photographer, whose shop used to be situated in the Market Square in Eyemouth. The fleet are marooned in the bay awaiting the tide to turn and the horses and carts are waiting to offload the catch from the ferrying 'punts'.

THE BAY AND FISHING FLEET, EYEMOUTH

11 Photographed from the north of the bay across the rocks at low tide you can clearly see the fleet of old steam drifters waiting for the tide to turn. This was obviously an extremely low tide and there is a lot of interest and business being conducted around the boats.

866. FISHING FLEET IN EYEMOUTH BAY.

12 This real photo postcard sent in 1916 shows how severe the sea and weather can be for the front of the town. Even although the Hurkar Rocks serve as a natural breakwater, the waves still pound in and the houses along the seaward side are inundated with water. The message on the postcard tells the story of watching 'a big ship by which the children say has been damaged by a submarine'. We forget that even during wartime, people still took holidays.

13 This very rare photograph is of a Yarmouth-registered fishing boat, which failed to negotiate the difficult entry into the safe haven of Eyemouth harbour. The 'Jacob George' was skippered by Andrew Dougal ('Old Youngster') and was driven onto the rocks and eventually wrecked. The crew was rescued by the local Coastguard and Lifeboat services by Breeches Buoy.

14   Shipwreck photographs are always very interesting. This is of the S.S. President which struck Whup Ness to the south of the last hole at Eyemouth Golf course. This coastal freighter was completely destroyed, but thankfully with no loss of life. Very little remains of her now and the broken and rusting plates are now festooned in all manner of marine life.

The Wreck at Whup Ness, Eyemouth.

15 As you will notice, this is also a post-1930 picture postcard but is of particular interest due to the contents. This German sea-plane crash landed in the bay in 1945. The pilot was saved and held captive by the local Home Guard. The aeroplane was soon dismantled by the locals. It was said that those who tried to use the fuel from the sea plane had a nasty surprise, it was too rich a mix for their tractor engines and they all blew-up!

16   This postcard sent in 1923 and tells: 'Norman is disgusted with Eyemouth as there are no shops to suit him!' Eyemouth is a coastal fishing village, whose whole aspect is formed around the sea. This view of the old pier head shows the wooden pilings driven into the sand to try and retain part of the land to use as a slipway. Concrete has one the day, eventually.

17   This is also a very old photograph of the entrance to Eyemouth harbour and photographed from the front of the lifeboat station in 1886. Here a horse and cart are led away from the harbour carrying the old hemp nets which will be spread out to dry before being loaded once more onto the sailing ships. Eyemouth's tightly-packed houses and smoking 'lums' can be seen quite clearly and the old set of steps leading down to the harbour are also long gone

18   This very interesting photograph shows the Eyemouth Lifeboat being rowed out to sea. It is uncertain whether she was off to rescue a boat in distress, or whether she was on exercise. The life boat station was opened in 1876 at a coast of £500 and then rebuilt in 1908 and a new slipway constructed at a further cost of £750. This photograph may be of the 'James and Rachel Grindley' or the 'Sarah Pickard', it is difficult to tell.

19 Trees are a rare sight in Eyemouth, in fact all the way up the east coast. These silver birch on the footpath towards Gunsgreen Mansion House forms a perfect frame for a view of the old Eyemouth harbour. The sailing yawls are anchored up, this was probably a Sunday, and the weather appears fine and the sea is calm.

20   This 'Guaranteed Real Photo and British Manufactured' postcard posted on 31st July 1930 has the writer intrigued about the secret passages in this old smuggler's house. The tower at the top of the hill is attributed to Oliver Cromwell and was supposedly built during his Scottish campaign. For many years it was used as a dovecoate for the big house.

MANSION HOUSE AND TOWER (B.) EYEMOUTH.

21 Gunsgreen House or the 'Mansion House' as it is known locally was the centre for Eyemouth's smuggling trade. The mock battlements in front of the house conceal huge storage caverns where the contraband was secured. Passageways connected the interior of the house to entrances in the caverns as well as several escape routes along the coast. There is many a fine wealthy local family who owe their fame and fortune to those smuggling days.

MANSION HOUSE (B.) EYEMOUTH.

22 This unused postcard is in absolute mint condition. It obviously dated from the turn of the century and even after all these years, I am constantly amazed at the condition of some of them. Here the yawls are crossing the 'bar', furling up their heavy cotton sails and rowing the remainder of the way in towards the fish market. A 'callant' sits watching from his punt, his work already done.

Crossing the Bar, Eyemouth

23   This is a beautifully-styled Art Nouveau picture postcard. A real photograph is sandwiched between the two halves of the card. The photograph is of the Berwickshire registered yawl the BK220 'Dauntless'. The message on the card says: 'Sent with Affection to Swell your Collection.'

24   This Brown's Series picture postcard is from 1903. It shows the extended middle pier and all the masts of the fishing fleet at rest. The tightly-packed houses, wynds and vennels can be seen in the background.

Brown's Series.

EYEMOUTH

I have not forgotten you.   M. Scott

25 A superb 'Real Photograph' from the turn of the century. The harbour is packed with fishing boats at low tide, unable to leave the harbour. The sides of the quay are filled with empty barrels awaiting the salted herring for shipment overseas.

26   A similar view to the previous postcard, but twenty years later. The sailing vessels have been replaced by steam and the decks are now enclosed. The herring barrels still line the quayside and this was the mainstay of the fishing fleet for many generations.

THE HARBOUR, EYEMOUTH.

27 The photographer A.R. Edwards from Selkirk was often in Eyemouth and his portraits of everyday scenes are much saught after in the Borders. At the end of the inner harbour is the slipway, still in use today next to the sluice gates, which could be opened when the river was in flood. Here a coastal freighter, billowing smoke from its coal boilers, is loading barrels of herring for shipment to the south. The high wall of Burgon's yard in the background is no longer there, now replaced by a car park.

28   This fine view of Eyecliffs is interesting. Boats are no longer pulled up alongside the riverbed. The footpath, known as the Bane Mill Brae, now leads up to the more modern housing estate. There are still cottages at this side of the river on the same site, the old buildings have long since been demolished. The house with smoke coming out of the chimney was formerly one of the toll houses, also gone.

29   This beautifully-worked marble memorial is in memory of the 129 Eyemouth men lost their lives during a terrible, sudden tempest on 14th October 1881. The fishing boats were unable to reach the safety of the harbour and before the storm died down, there were left 107 widows and 351 orphans. Twenty fishing boats were destroyed within sight of the shore, some of the men only an arm's length from safety.

30 This Valentine's Series' card from 1906 is photographed outside the 'Hippodrome'. The fish were landed wherever there was space on the quayside in olden days. Fish markets still attract a great deal of attention and the auctioneer is always interesting to listen to.

A Fish Auction, Eyemouth

Valentines Series

31   There is no fish curing in Eyemouth anymore, only smoke houses. The original salt curing process was invented in the time of King Alexander III in the thirteenth century. Here the fisher lassies are preparing the herring before they are packed into barrels for export.

654. FISH CURING. EYEMOUTH.

32   This excellent postcard is of the 'fisher lads and lassies' who followed the herring fleet as they in turn followed the shoals of herring. This postcard is probably from Great Yarmouth, but it shows the crew employed by the fish merchant John Burgon. This business is still in operation today.

33   Another group of young fish workers, their 'peenies' covered in fish guts and scales. Piece workers were paid 8 shillings a week and between 6d or 8d for each barrel packed. Selected barrels would hold approximately 850 herring. This was akin to a type of slave trade, because there was no Factory Act enforced for workers on the quay.

34 A splendid postcard of the old Toll Bridge, the Toll House and the 'Prefabs'. Everything is gone now. The bridge over the old railway line has been replaced, the Toll House demolished and the 'prefabs' finally ungraded into a modern housing development. This is now a busy road and mothers would not dare to walk down the middle of the road pushing a pram nowadays.

Looking across Toll Brig, Eyemouth.

35   This picture postcard from 1909 shows the toll houses at either side of the old Toll Bridge. The houses stood until the 1930's, when they were finally demolished. This house to the right was opposite the entrance to Netherbyres.

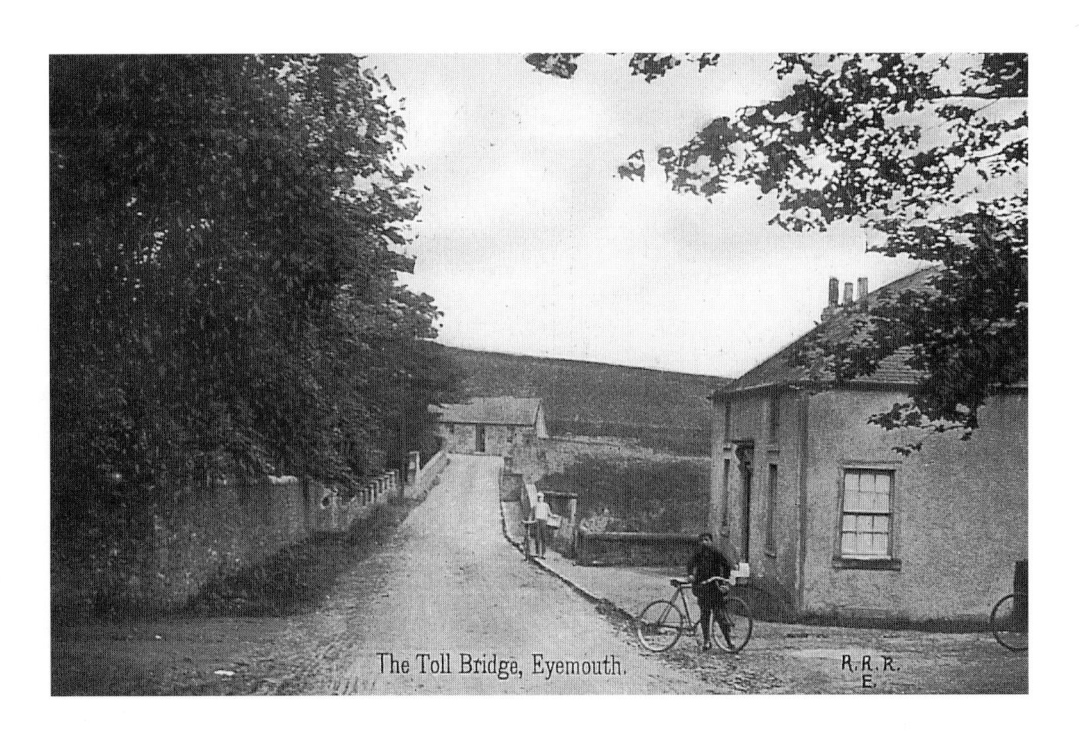

The Toll Bridge, Eyemouth.

36   Another picture postcard produced by J. Parker from Eyemouth. This small bridge was destroyed during the flood of 1948 and replaced by the 'silver bridge'. This picture postcard was sent in 1929, the writer was having a 'jolly time'.

WOODEN BRIDGE, EYEMOUTH

37   A very rare old photograph again from Mr. Parker. This is actually of the edge of the riverbank before the railway line and station were built. Even the houses along Victoria Road have not all been built. This area of the riverside proved to be the best location for the station.

38   This view of the Old Toll Bridge shows the single span of the river and the railway track also passing underneath to the right-hand side. The original intention for the terminus of the railway was to place it up on the field above where Gilsland housing estate is now. However, the railway authority decided to place the station down next to the river mouth behind the harbour with the hope that they would be able to extend the railway track onto the quay.

39   The railway track travelled all the way up hill to Burnmouth and the River Eye had to be crossed near Millbank. The viaduct was constructed to cross the river and the line was elevated to 60 feet above the riverbed. There were six 50 ft wrought-iron lattice girder spans, supported on four-sided brick-faced concrete piers. When the station finally closed, the railway track was lifted and now the only reminder left are the brick piers, still standing.

40 This is a particularly detailed view of Eyemouth Railway Station. The original intention of the railway company was to extend the track onto the quay, but unfortunately they could not afford to buy the large house which stood in their way. The railway and station had to remain where it was and the local fishermen had to transport their fish by horse and cart up to the station for loading onto the train.

EYEMOUTH FROM THE RIVER

41 The station and platform were officially opened on 13th April 1891. The station consisted of a platform, booking-office and loading bay, while on the track, a crossover road led from the passenger line to one of the two sidings. In 1895 and again in 1900 alterations were made to the station adding a weigh house and weigh bridge, moving same and adding another siding leading to a goods shed. It was believed that the 1900 alterations had to be carried out because the original station was destroyed in a fire.

42   The Eyemouth Harbour Trust tried repeatedly for twelve years to gain the land it needed to extend the line onto the harbour and rebuild the now totally inadequate station. Sadly the finance was not able to be justified and the station stayed as it was until its closure on 5th February 1962. This fine old photograph is taken from the top of the road looking down into the station. All the goods freight travelled along this road.

43   In 1913 just before the outbreak of war 25,593 passengers used the line bringing in a revenue of £2,498; freight charges amounted to £1,628. By 1920, 34,798 passengers used the line and a single ticket from Burnmouth cost threepence and it cost fivepence return. When she closed in 1962, the last fare cost 1/6 return and 2/4 to travel first class to Burnmouth. This view also shows the old Bone Mill situated above the river.

44   This view looking along Albert Road also shows the entrance to Eyemouth School House, which has now been demolished to build a day-care centre as an addition to Eyemouth Health Centre. The old gas lamps are very much in evidence and the wide thoroughfares are uncluttered by cars!

ALBERT ROAD LOOKING N, EYEMOUTH.

45   This is a splendid picture postcard of the teachers in service in Eyemouth School. They are, from the back, left to right: May Gray, Maggie Bell, Isa Crystal, Kitty Borthwick, Jeannie Collin, May Armitage, Miss Smith, Maggie Donaldson, Miss McLennon, Mr. McDowell, Miss Kerr, Miss Gordon, Mr. Chalmers, Mr. McGrouther and Maggie Blackie. The card was sent to Miss M. G. Craig in Albert Road to remind her 'in the dim and distant future of the two beauties when they have left her behind.'

46   Further along Albert Road is an oddly-shaped corner house. This very old postcard shows James Crawford, who was the young boy, and the older lady is Madge Craig. The house became a shop and was used by 'Alec the Pole' as a watch and clock repairers. This part of the building now belongs to Alistair Scott, who has been a great help over the years and is an absolute mine of information on Eyemouth's history.

47   This is a very early view of Seafield in Eyemouth, looking up towards its junction with Coldingham Road. Could that be a model T Ford on the road?

Seafield, Eyemouth.

48 Up above and behind Seafield were the tennis courts. Playing tennis was and still is a popular pastime in the town and it was mentioned in quite a number of early postcards. As you can see, there are no other houses in behind the first row. The whole area is completely built up now and has been for many years.

TENNIS COURTS, EYEMOUTH.

49   This is another of J. Parker's picture postcards and is of Upper Houdlaw. This very early photograph has the bottom row of houses only and the pavement. This abuts directly onto a green field, no road.

50   At the bottom of Coldingham Road, at the junction of Albert Road and Victoria Road, stands the Glenerne Hotel. This is still one of only a small handful of hotels in the town and this postcard, obviously specifically produced for the Glenerne, shows a happy group of residents enjoying the afternoon sun.

51   The other main hotel back in the nineteen twenties and thirties was the Home Arms Hotel on the High Street. This lovely old picture postcard was posted in 1930 and shows the influence of the motor car already. The RAC sign is hanging on the wall. Cobbled streets of course and the old cemetery is next door.

52   Commerce Street continued from the vennel between the Hippodrome and the Ship Hotel, connecting onto George Wynd and George Street at the top of the postcard. This was one of the main thoroughfares used by the fishermen when taking their baited lines and 'lintrays' to the harbour. Nothing exists of Commerce Street or George Wynd. The buildings have long gone and are now replaced by Swan Court. There is still a footpath access through the bottom of the vennel next to the Ship Hotel.

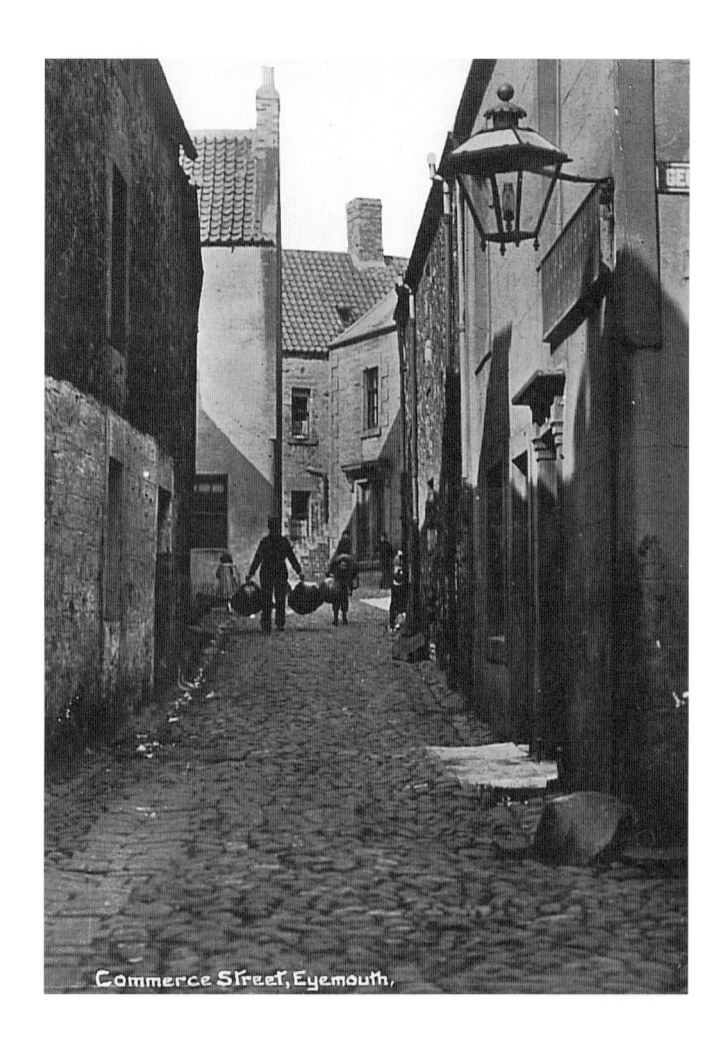

53   Looking in the opposite direction from the Market Square up Church Street, we can see at once that the new road down towards the harbour has been responsible for the demolition of many fine old buildings. The local 'bairns' were obviously intrigued by the very rare sight of a photographer.

Church Street, Eyemouth

54   A very old view of the High Street as seen from the Market Square. At one time there used to be two annual fairs held in the town's Market Square. These were on the first Thursday in June and the last Thursday in October. Games and sports were also played on the Fort Point. These included hammer-throwing, ball-putting and foot-racing. Sadly the market eventually ceased, but the tradition of exchanging gifts on the last Thursday of October continued for many years. Even that is forgotten now.

High Street, Eyemouth

55   A much later postcard of the Market Square and produced by M. Collin of 1 High Street, Eyemouth. More vehicular traffic now and a lamp-post and keep left sign have been placed in the centre of the Square. The butcher's shop was originally owned by my grandfather W. Dougal or 'Brasso', as he was known in the town.

56   Opposite 'Brasso's' shop was Dougal's. This family business is still in existance today, but the shop has undergone many changes. Here, Mr. Dougal stands proudly in front of his new delivery van. Much of the storage space still used by the shop was originally smugglers' cellars and connected many of the town's buildings which were quite close to Eyemouth harbour.

57   This is a lovely old picture postcard of the Red Hills. This public footpath is much favoured by the townspeople as they walk towards Killiedraughts Bay and onwards to Lincum Beach and Coldingham Sands. The field directly behind the two people enjoying the view is dominated by Northburn Holiday Home Park, owned and operated by the Wood family. The walk 'roond the braes' was described as early as the eighteenth century as being a tonic to city people.

58   This is a lovely old photograph sent in 1908 of the Lodge at the southern entrance to Netherbyres House, the former home of Lt. Colonel Furness. The Lodge is also long gone, it is sad to see so much of the old town disappear. Quaint old buildings, so much a part of our heritage, should always be preserved.

Netherbyres Lodge, Eyemouth.

59   This very fine old picture postcard was posted in 1906, but the photograph itself is much older. Virtually nothing remains of this mill, further up the river Eye. There was also an old paper mill at Millbank, in between Ayton and Eyemouth. This was totally destroyed by fire in 1869 after being in operation for 61 years. A paper mill still exists, using the waters of Berwickshire. This is now situated outside Chirnside.

60 Very close to the position of the old mill was Maggie Murphy's Cottage. Situated on a rather tight corner on the Eyemouth side of Mill Bank, it stood for many years. Sadly the building fell into total disrepair and the roof was finally removed several years ago. The shell is a constant reminder to the changes to this part of the east coast of Scotland.

61　Multiple view cards were always very popular with collectors. It also gave the receiver a much better appreciation for the town it was sent from. Here we see six views of Eyemouth. Each view was also produced as a separate postcard. The only one I am yet to locate is the one of the Bowling Green situated just off Coldingham Road. Bowling is still very popular in the town and one of Eyemouth's lady members was selected to play in the Commonwealth Games.

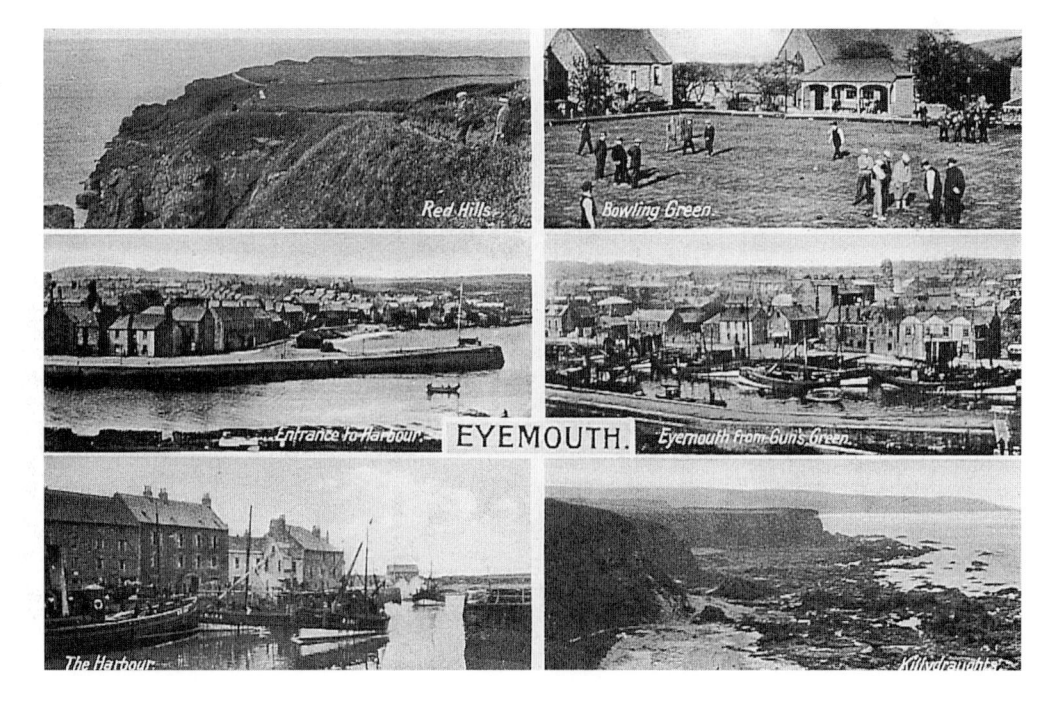

62   A delightful card of a few 'bairns' baithing down on the foreshore at Burnmouth. Dated around 1909, the children are playing around the callants' punts.

Bathing.

M. Wane & Co., Edinbro', No. 34.

63 The Burnmouth and Berwickshire registered herring boat or Fyfie, the Nellie Wilson BK102, is seen here at the harbour in Great Yarmouth. The fishermen were often gone for months on end, following the shoals of 'silver darlings'. The boats were primarily used during the summer months and at the turn of the century averaged between 55 to 69 feet in length. Most of the fishing boats were built at Weatherheads in Eyemouth and a boat of this size would cost in the region £600 (not including nets).

64   This is a lovely old card of lower Burnmouth. The only way of getting to the three smaller hamlets is down a steep winding road from the Station. The trouble of the descent is amply compensated for by the view. It has the appearance of a 'Cornish' village.

65   This is also a particularly fine old picture postcard of Lower Burnmouth. An everyday scene, somewhat posed for the photographer. The villagers also appear to be in their Sunday best.

66   This is one of the best picture postcards produced by A.R. Edwards of Selkirk, perhaps one of the most prolific of all the local photographers. This is a very fine photograph of Burnmouth Station at the turn of the century. The passengers appear to be waiting on the northbound train. The photograph is rare because it has two trains in the frame. The railway line to the left was used by the Eyemouth train.

THE STATION, BURNMOUTH.

67   Lamberton Toll on the Border between Scotland and England. Nothing of these original buildings remain. Hailed as Gretna Green of the Eastern Marches, Lamberton was even more popular for runaway marriages. The identical Temple of Hymen and the old blacksmith's shop used to stand witness to a romantic age, sadly it is all gone now, in favour of a dual carriageway. It is hoped that there will be a new cross border development in the future – with perhaps another marriage house!

68 I have decided to include this rather quaint view from the school in Ayton. Ayton is Eyemouth's other sister town and now largely forgotten, due to the bypassing of the town by the A1 Trunk Road. This wonderful old picture postcard shows the school children in what must have been a very difficult pose for the photographer.

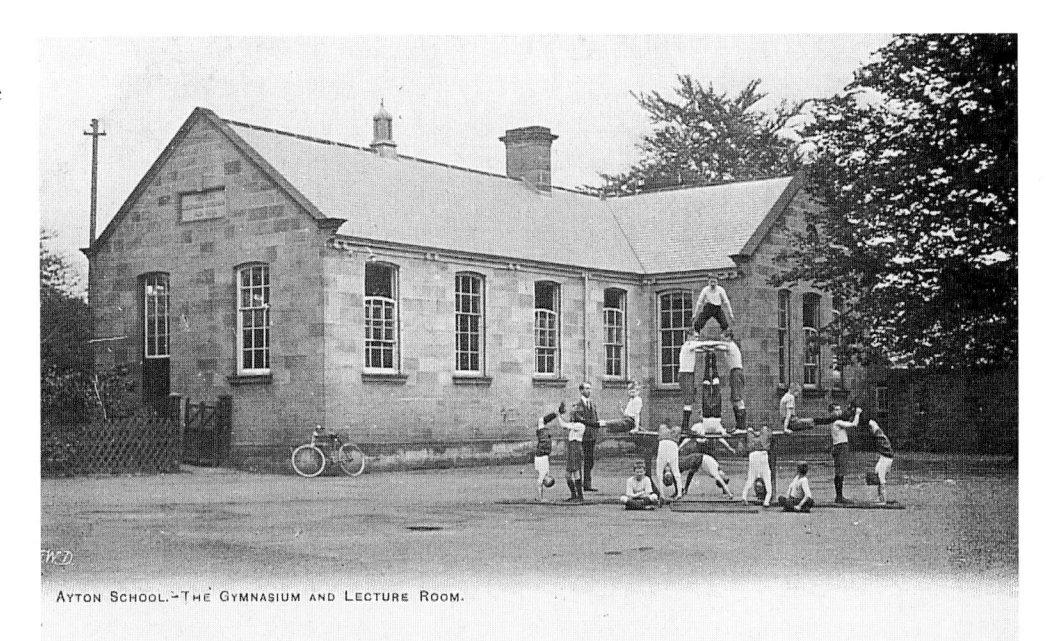

AYTON SCHOOL.—THE GYMNASIUM AND LECTURE ROOM.

69 Coldingham Village Square, again photographed by A.R. Edwards of Selkirk. The Anchor Inn is still in the town and there is now a garage where the old carts are standing. Horseless carriages were soon to come to this quiet village.

70   Coldingham Priory still dominates Coldingham Village. As far back as the seventh century there was a monastic settlement on Coldburgh (now St. Abbs Head) and in 1098 Coldingham Priory was founded by King Edgar. It was originally called the church of St. Mary Coldingham and it was constituted as a cell of Durham. In 1509 it was disjoined from Durham and placed under the jurisdiction of Dunfermline by the Pope. In 1545 it was burned to the ground by the Earl of Hertford and further destroyed by Cromwell leaving only the north wall and east gable. It was finally repaired in 1831 and the church is still used to this day.

The Priory.   *Coldingham.*

I was here on Sunday morning.

1280. 61. Albany Series.

71   This is a very rare picture postcard posted in Ayton on 23rd August 1905 to Reston, only a couple of miles away! This is a view of Pilgrims on the shore of Coldingham Bay holding the Service of the Sea. Coldingham Beach is one of the top beaches in Europe today.

72   This very rare photograph dates from around 1918, but is not clarified. What you see is a helium, hydrogen or air balloon which was used by the Royal Navy as a 'lifting bag' to float a small boat from the sea bed off Coldingham Bay. The balloon is now deflated and you can see the boat quite clearly. The writing on the Humbie Knowe (the small round hill behind) says: 'Hill 60. Mons St. Eloi, Ypres, Loos, Somme, Mone.' The balloon had the number C6 on its side and was accompanied by a frigate. Nothing is known of the incident, can anyone help?

73   This is a very fine postcard produced by Robert Nisbet, who was formerly the postmaster at St. Abbs. St. Abbs is named after Ebba, daughter of one of the King's of Northumberland, who established a nunnery on the headland in the eighth century. A small harbour was first built at Northfield Shore in 1833 at a cost of £1,200 and sixteen families lived close by. In the accounts of 1834, they tell of fourteen fishing boats using the harbour and their catches being transported in carts to the markets in Edinburgh. This view of Briery Law shows the row of houses behind Rock House, which have now been completely demolished. This used to be known as Under Row.

74   This splendid postcard gives you the sensation of what hard lives these fishermen faced as they tended their boats, baited their lines and scraped a living from the bountiful sea. The men are holding hemp ropes and crans which were used for measuring the specific weight of herrings. The village was known as Coldingham Shore until 1892, when it became known as St. Abbs. That year the Free Church was also erected, a gift of Andrew Usher Esq.

75   Lifeboat No. 603, the 'Helen Smitten' was launched at St. Abbs Harbour on 25th April 1911. She was a legacy of Mr. James Hodge of Manchester and cost £3,563. She was stationed as a direct result of the sinking of the Alfred Earlandson on the Ebb Carrs. She was launched 27 times, saved 37 lives and served the village until 1936. The postcard was posted from St. Abbs on 2nd September 1912. The lifeboat is now of the inshore variety and has a covered shed in the position directly behind where the lifeboat is situated on the slipway, ready to be launched.

Launch of St. Abbs Lifeboat.

76   This, the last picture postcard in this second volume, is of the S.S. Mauritania undergoing her sea trials off St. Abbs Head. The lighthouse was first opened in 1862 and was continually manned until just a few years ago. Once more technology has overtaken tradition and the lighthouse is now fully automated. The sight of this steam ship with her distinctive four funnels must have been quite breathtaking.